The Argument of Innocence

The Argument of Innocence

A Selection from the Arts of
Kenneth Patchen

Text by Peter Veres
Foreword by Miriam Patchen

The Scrimshaw Press
1976

To Ruth, Maia and Michael
  —with special thanks to Miriam Patchen
    for her patient help and friendship.

Text copyright © 1976 by Peter Veres
Illustrations copyright © 1976 by Miriam Patchen

Library of Congress Cataloging in Publication Data

Patchen, Kenneth, 1911–1972.
  The argument of innocence.

  Bibliography: p.
  1. Patchen, Kenneth, 1911–1972. I. Veres, Peter,
1938–   II. Title.
N6537.P27V47   709′.2′4   75-9695
ISBN 0-912020-39-3

Thanks to Random House, Inc. for their permission to reprint an Apollinaire
  quote from Roger Shattuck's *The Banquet Years* © 1955, 1957, 1958 by
  Roger Shattuck.
Special thanks are due to New Directions Publishing Co. for their very generous
  permission to quote from various Patchen titles. Our reproductions of the
  "The Orange Bears," "Joe Hill Listens to the Praying," and "Class of 1934"
  are taken directly from *The Collected Poems of Kenneth Patchen,*
  New Directions, 1968.

The Scrimshaw Press
6040 Claremont Avenue
Oakland
California 94618

Foreword

A NYONE WHO ATTEMPTS to discuss the works of Kenneth Patchen labors under his admonition, "It's all in my books." And, to be sure, so it is. The essence of the man, what he said and what he meant, is all in his writing.

Kenneth Patchen does not fit any neat stereotype of the artist. There was nothing either precious or dissolute about him. He was a positive person. Whether the task at hand was his studies, or football, or hammering a nail, he knew he could do it—and do it well he did. The same attitude prevailed in his creative efforts. Everything he wanted to do, until physical illness deterred him, he did. His words flowed onto his paper without changes. His paintings and drawings needed no alterations or corrections. Kenneth Patchen knew what had to be done, and did it. His entire life, from his childhood until his death, was spent, totally, in creative activity.

He was always traveling onward, trying to expand and tighten his meanings and methods. The picture poems are a strong example. Had a little more physical strength been left, a little more time, he would have succeeded in solving the problems on which he was working. Failing that, he still managed to chart new ways highly pleasing for us to journey along.

As John Frederick Nims says in his *Western Wind,* "The vitality of Patchen's vocabulary is clear if we contrast his page with a page of words that are dead or close to dying." It is the "dead or close to dying" that Kenneth Patchen spent a lifetime

5

to overcome, as more and more of the world's words approached a state for embalming. He loved words—their sounds, their rhythms, their true meanings. They, of course, take on individual meanings and connotations for each reader, just as a person will be known differently to each of his friends. Patchen was constantly trying to keep connotation and meaning, to bring those words up, off the page, out of the book.

These attempts took many forms. The final plateau became the picture poems. The paintings are not illustrations. The words are not separate from the graphics accompanying them. They must be experienced together. Complementing each other, they convey the sense and feeling of the whole work.

My deepest thanks are due to Peter Veres, without whom this project would not have come about. His long and diligent efforts have at last made it possible to play the score with full orchestra, not just one instrument. So, too, am I indebted to the Scrimshaw Press for their willingness to publish the picture poems in color and for a belief that good work, well presented, will find a responsive audience.

Kenneth Patchen, like Apollinaire before him, opened windows. Now it remains for others to continue along the line of expanding visual communications.

MIRIAM PATCHEN
1975

6

Introduction

EXCEPT FOR CERTAIN ANTS, man is the only creature which engages entire societies in planning and carrying out large-scale warfare against its own kind. The twentieth century has been dominated by the vastest undertaking of destructive activity in the history of our species; all aspects of human life—social and individual, physical and spiritual—have been touched in some way by the forces of homicide.

Anger and outrage at those who make war are at the heart of the work of Kenneth Patchen. He was, above all, a moral writer with a love and respect for life. In an era of expediency and compromise, of patriotic rhetoric and intellectual aestheticism, he did *not* simply accept what he witnessed, nor did he find escape into some neutral mental sphere, but he cried out in the wilderness of greed and cruelty "against all enemies of life."

In his poetry, prose and picture poems, Patchen faced the ancient conflict between good and evil, between life and death, and unequivocally took his stand. Thou shalt not kill, maim, torture, enslave, exploit, nor otherwise oppress—there are no exceptions. Thou *shalt* love and honor life, freedom, and imagination—thou shalt give joy. He knew that the two energies coexist, that the evil threatens and sometimes overwhelms the good, but he believed that life—the good—would prevail (because it must). That was Kenneth Patchen's driving, encompassing vision in his life and in his life's work.

> You will be told that what I write is confused, without order—and I tell you that my book is not concerned with the problems of art, but with the problems of this world, with the problems of life itself—yes, of *life itself.*
> *(The Journal of Albion Moonlight)*

"Life itself" is complex and multileveled, with conflicts and contradictions often juxtaposed or overlapping in our experiences. Patchen developed the techniques of his art as the means of achieving a language strong enough, clear enough, to embody a living presentation of his vision—beyond clichés, sentimentality, obscure symbolisms, or aesthetic formalism.

To bring into focus the disparate elements of a time out of joint (and to include the essence of their disjunction), Patchen developed a poetry of multiformity and interfusion. Moving beyond the use of traditional typesetting techniques, he explored the possibilities of contrast in the *look* of words on a page, experimenting with various combinations of placement, type sizes, unusual typefaces, and, eventually, with the inclusion of nonverbal marks and imagery in his writing.

Patchen's graphics—his visual work—originated in his writing, not as illustration of a text but as amplification of the poet's medium, a reintegration of word and image, a personal vision made truly visible to the reader.

While Patchen's picture poems give form to a unique and highly personal vision, their heritage dates back to medieval manuscripts. The early monastic scribes embellished their calligraphy with ornate capital letters, often intertwined with fantastic animal forms as well as human figures. These figures were, in time, separated from their calligraphic contexts and were given their own place in the book as illuminated scenes, illustrating and augmenting the text. These pictures became a source of the naturalistic painting that for centuries characterized western European art.

A few poets, dating at least from William Blake, have given back to words their visual power as graphic signs—beyond their aural essence of sound and meaning, even integrating non-calligraphic imagery within the limits of the universe of the page. In our own times, the French poet Guillaume Apollinaire, the Italian futurist poets, and the whole international movement of Dada painter-poets, successively developed works which explored the shapes and placement of the written word and the relationship between the meaning of a poem and its appearance on the page.

In twentieth-century art we have seen a powerful movement to expand formal vocabularies as means of expression. All of the arts have been broken up and reassembled. Simultaneity and juxtaposition, elements taken out of ordinary context, are some of the devices used to expand formal expressive means, from the first cubist collages to surrealist painting and poetry. In Surrealism, an important tactical procedure was that of disorienting the conscious processes of the reader's mind through methods of chance. Torn bits of paper, assembled at random—freely improvised graphic marks—could suggest new and unexpected associations of meaning, capable of building a new reality. Patchen was thoroughly familiar with the work of the poets who preceded him and also acutely conscious of the pressures and qualities of life around him. He built his art in response to the circumstances of that life through his personal adaptation and development of its language. His growth found its ultimate form in the picture poems.

8

Written Works

KENNETH PATCHEN BEGAN writing poetry as a boy in the iron-and-steel town of Warren, in northeastern Ohio, five miles down the Mahoning River from Niles, where he had been born, the second son of a steelworker, on December 13, 1911.

The Orange Bears

The orange bears with soft friendly eyes
Who played with me when I was ten,
Christ, before I left home they'd had
Their paws smashed in the rolls, their backs
Seared by hot slag, their soft trusting
Bellies kicked in, their tongues ripped
Out, and I went down through the woods
To the smelly crick with Whitman
In the Haldeman-Julius edition,
And I just sat there worrying my thumbnail
Into the cover—What did he know about
Orange bears with their coats all stunk up with soft coal
And the National Guard coming over
From Wheeling to stand in front of the millgates
With drawn bayonets jeering at the strikers?

I remember you could put daisies
On the windowsill at night and in
The morning they'd be so covered with soot
You couldn't tell what they were anymore.

A hell of a fat chance my orange bears had!

After high school, where he excelled both in scholarship and in competitive athletics, Patchen spent two summers working in the steel mills, a year at Alexander Meiklejohn's experimental college at the University of Wisconsin, and a short time at Commonwealth College in Mena, Arkansas. Then, in 1930, at the age of eighteen, he hit the road. For four years during the Great Depression he was on the move, doing odd jobs across a country abundant with natural beauty and impoverished humans trying to survive the harvest of corporate mismanagement and greed. Patchen's politics were formed in the time of capitalism's social collapse, before the economic revival of the Second World War. In 1934, Kenneth Patchen, poet and social critic, and Miriam Oikemus, a student and antiwar organizer, met and married. He was twenty-two and she was seventeen. They moved to New York, where they were to live, almost continuously, until 1947.

Joe Hill Listens to the Praying

Look at the steady rifles, Joe.
It's all over now . . . "Murder, first degree,"
The jury said. It's too late now
To go back. Listen Joe, the chaplain is reading:

Lord Jesus Christ who didst
So mercifully promise heaven
To the thief that humbly confessed
His injustice
                throw back your head
Joe; remember that song of yours
We used to sing in jails all over
These Benighted States . . . tell it to him:
"I'll introduce to you
A man that is a credit to our Red, White
and Blue,
His head is made of lumber and solid as
a rock;
He is a Christian Father and his name is
Mr. Block."
                Remember, Joe—
"You take the cake,
You make me ache,
Tie a rock on your block and jump
in the lake,
Kindly do that for Liberty's sake."

Behold me, I beseech Thee, with
The same eyes of mercy that
                     on the other
Hand we're driftin' into Jungles

From Kansas to the coast, wrapped
        round brake beams on a thousand
        freights; San Joaquin and Omaha
        brush under the wheels—"God made the sun
        for the hobo and the bummer"—we've been
        everywhere, seen everything.
Winning the West for the good citizens;
Driving golden spikes into the U.P.;
Harvest hands, lumbermen drifting—
        now Iowa, now Oregon—
God, how clean the sky; the lovely wine
Of coffee in a can. This land
        is our lover. How greenly beautiful
Her hair; her great pure breasts
        that are
The Rockies on a day of mist and rain.

We love this land of corn and cotton,
        Virginia and Ohio, sleeping on
With our love, with our love—
O burst of Alabama loveliness, sleeping on
In the strength of our love; O Mississippi flowing
Through our nights, a giant mother.

Pardon, and in the end
        How green is her hair,
        how pure are her breasts; the little farms
        nuzzling into her flanks
        drawing forth life, big rich life
Under the deep chant of her skies
And rivers—but we, we're driftin'
Into trouble from Kansas to the coast, clapped
        into the stink and rot of country jails
        and clubbed by dicks and cops
Because we didn't give a damn—
                    remember Joe
How little we cared, how we sang
        the nights away in their filthy jails;
                 and how, when
We got wind of a guy called Marx
        we sang less, just talked
And talked. "Blanket-stiffs" we were
But we could talk, they couldn't jail us
For that—but they did—

                      remember Joe
Of my life be strengthened
                      One Big Union:
          our convention in Chi; the Red Cards,
          leaflets; sleeping in the parks,
          the Boul' Mich; "wobblies" now, cheering
          the guys that spoke our lingo, singing
          down the others. "Hear that train blow,
Boys, hear that train blow."

Now confessing my crimes, I may obtain

Millions of stars, Joe—millions of miles

                      Remember Vincent St. John
In the Goldfield strike; the timid little squirt
          with the funny voice, getting onto the platform
          and slinging words at us that rolled
          down our chins and into our hearts,
          like boulders hell-bent down a mountain side.
And Orchard, angel of peace
          —with a stick of dynamite in either hand.
          Pettibone and Moyer: "The strike
Is your weapon, to hell with politics."
                      Big Bill—remember him—
At Boise—great red eye rolling like a lame bull's
          through the furniture and men
          of the courtroom—"This bastard,
His Honor."
          Yeah!
          Hobo Convention:
(Millions of stars, Joe—millions of miles.)
"Hallelujah, I'm a bum,
Hallelujah, I'm a bum." His Honor,
          the sonofabitch!
One Big Strike, Lawrence, Mass.—
          23,000 strong, from every neck
          of every woods in America, 23,000,
Joe, remember. "We don't need
          a leader. We'll fix things up
          among ourselves."
"Blackie" Ford and "Double-nose" Suhr in

12

Wheatland—"I.W.W.'s don't destroy
                property"—and they got life. "I've counted
The stars, boys, counted a million of these prison bars."
                Yeah!
                San Diego, soap boxes,
Hundreds of them! And always
                their jail shutting out the sky,
                the clean rhythm of the wheels
                on a fast freight; disinfectant getting
                into the lung-pits, spitting blood
But singing—Christ, how we sang,
                                        remember the singing
Joe, One Big Union,
                One Big
                        hope to be
With Thee

What do they matter, Joe, these massed rifles—
They can't reach the towns, the skies, the songs,
                that now are part of more
                than any of us—we were
The homeless, the drifters, but our songs
                had hair and blood on them.

There are no soap boxes in the sky.
We won't eat pie, now, or ever
                when we die,
                        but Joe
We had something they didn't have:
                our love for these States
                was real and deep;
                                to be with Thee
In heaven. Amen.
                (How steady are
the rifles.) We had slept
                naked on this earth on the coldest nights
                listening to the words of a guy named Freedom.
Let them burn us, hang us, shoot us,
                                Joe Hill,
For at the last we had what it takes
                to make songs with.

Before the Brave, Patchen's first book of poems, was published in 1936, in the first year of the Spanish Civil War. By the time his next book, *First Will & Testament,* appeared in 1939, all of Europe was at war—again. Tidings of death, suffering, and madness accompanied Patchen's journey in the development of his art.

Many of Patchen's enduring themes are contained in his poem "Class of 1934": lovers in the beauty of the natural world ("remember that night in the hills? the moon the stars . . .") who are bloodily destroyed; the merchants of death—Hitler, Morgan, Hoover, Mussolini; the "well-fed politicians" of all sides and all countries, who order out the armies of the young to kill and be killed, who starve the poor and kill the union picket in San Francisco. The other theme, the voice of promise of a reality beyond the chaos *(in the heavens high Above you stars and within you sky. . . Where bright angel feet have trod)* is heard only sparingly in this poem. There is faith, in the face of all horror, that life will ultimately triumph over the forces of death ("We cannot fail").

Class of 1934

Say something, man, say something before the nations and
    the people;
tell them your story tell them the earth is a bitch gone crazy.
Explain the joke the shadow-days explain the troops and guns
        get down on your knees young men   What happened
to your girl? remember that night in the hills? the moon
    the stars
her face her lips   bloodily   What did you promise? what
    did you do?
        gentlemen I offer two dollars I offer bread and a blue
dress with puffed sleeves *Once the weight and fate of Europe
hung* her eyes were bright and dreamful larger than life
                        when they
cut her down (stop it kill him swing it sister swing it over
the limb of a tall tree where they can't get honeysuckle
    good night
God will guide you a gull will take you home) when they took
the automatic out of her hand when they met her on the street
        offering two dollars

Sin can never taint you now with the rocketflare the scream white
and holy eyeballs crimson shot with fire O mongrel froth of cities
being blasted to bits O vulgar little men operating beautiful in-
struments

14

bringing the blue restless sky down into their eyes not
seeing not knowing not caring O my god my god where did they
go   better to die better to feel that all wisdom science and mastery
have been turned against you that they notice you and kill you
(with the newspaper here on the desk beside me

        tell them Joe tell them Ed tell them I read about
        pale-green bells in a beautiful book having the face
of a happy man on its cover) better to die while heavy
    guns shake
the earth and it's all big and clear   save us from
    the peace between
wars   Fool fool every man's at war who's hungry
    and hunted whether
in Omaha or Tokyo here they come. Here they come Look out
they mean business they mean an end to standing in rain waiting
    for freights out of Toledo and Detroit Did we ever make
a town? a porterhouse? we were always just this side
    of getting anything
or anywhere

        Down on our luck down on your knees O villages of
terror and the soft slow ping of a 32 and the sure happy grind of
teeth in the head of a picket shot down in San Francisco. Chinese
children have little faces and the sky over China is blue as gun-
smoke as lovely as memory of good food   beardless boys
        in the Nineteenth Route Army love flowers and taffy
they wonder at the joke but they do not laugh multitudes harvest
rice and the bombing planes sound like bees   *O thou that dwell'st*
in the heavens high Above you stars and within you sky   mad
after spotless lilies   5:5:3: 1.75: 1.75:   British American Japanese
        French Italian battleships cruisers submarines torpedo-
boats *There were ninety and nine* listening to the man on the
radio Death Death
the retail price on cotton wheat and corn was
        Down on your knees
shells grenades bunting legs bayonets arms

more than two dollars   offers a chance

We present gas
Hitler offers
Death Death

steel helmets parade before the cells they twist his arms his testicles
Do you believe? Do you believe?

This is

the strain the eternal strain the Lord of all things loves Billy bully
Billy Hearst   barbed wire a crown of homos sharpshooters

"though

I cannot be a soldier, I can encourage them by dying"   Shanghai's
Big Sword Corps proves the cheering   1929 October 24 in every
pot a chicken a pot in every belly Morgan Hoover Mussolini   come
to bury them not to   Down on your knees   Palazzo Venezia
watch the stairs I'm coming up Watch that guy in the gray suit
thou dearest Augustine all is gone gone gone. What did they
say when you told them *Where bright angel feet have trod*
They said O.

We don't want much we want everything and the sun
withers the grass in the parks From our benches we can
see the stone faces of well-fed politicians we can hear
the doors close in Packards we can smell the perfume
of fat bitches with poodles   we can leave our benches we cannot
leave what they have done to us   we can stand up Christ we can
stand up in their highest building and we won't have room for all
the standing up we need   we've been under We've been nothing
We've been around too long they can't take us in They haven't
got a jail stout enough to hold us

they haven't

got a leg to stand on   Fool fool   just across the street
over those windows see their hard faces curl of cigarette
smoke above the machine guns   we're in the line of fire
they knock down good dough keeping us in line keeping us off Are they afraid are they sleeping less?

You're damn tootin'   but he said we don't
want much We want everything. A hundred million of
us coming

16

up those stairs in Spain in Mexico in India   O Father Abraham
puny business men reading newspapers thinking to tell us
        down on your knees!
                          Brothers! Brothers!
our hands in the sky in the sea in the earth making things grow
shut off the power shut off the power bridges roads tunnels trolleys
our factories our farms   What's the answer?   when you're down
on your knees with your mouth stuffed with worn-out views? lazy
bastards without the courage to see the deepringing beauty left to
us without the guts or heart to march in millions keeping step
with all that's gone before   making it live making it ours   O
huge epic time men
          up from your knees your books your prisoncots Avenge
your girl your youth   make them pay
                        where it hurts O earth
lovely tonight because of hope and stars and love
                    because of millions ready
to break the back of this muddle-born world
Young men
We must not fail.
We cannot fail.

The poem moves, driving forward, its various elements acting as both cause and effect of the momentum, contributing to the rush as well as caught up in its current. Multiplicity of details, of tones, of section lengths and rhythms, rush upon one another in continuous conflict and disorder, in interrupted and broken fragments of the story of humanity when "the earth is a bitch gone crazy." The effect is close to that of a film montage, with the pace of an intense newsreel, a medium Patchen referred to in a poem about the war in Cuba, "Leaflet (One)" from *Before the Brave:*

        What is the price of sugar? we view the work
        of high-powered rifles on the screen · "Machado
        has withdrawn." We flee the theater knowing
        they'll get us · they'll get us everyone

The real and the reel interact. In "Class of 1934" Patchen pointed to the mass media, the newspapers and radio, as a source of information as well as a form of structuring language:

> radio Death Death
> the retail price on cotton wheat and corn was
> >   Down on your knees
> shells grenades bunting legs bayonets arms
>
> more than two dollars   offers a chance
> >>   We present gas
> >>   Hitler offers
> >>   Death Death

Bits of information are interwoven, the placements both incongruous and significant. The cotton, wheat and corn markets need support from the legs and arms market; death buys gas. This structure of intercut elements presents the complex and multiple aspects of the world simultaneously rather than serially.

Patchen's later use of the graphic elements of typography and the other visual elements in his poetry grew out of and expanded this vision of conflicting forces and values. With *Before the Brave,* his first published book, he placed himself in the tradition of the European avant-garde, which had been involved, since late in the nineteenth century, with the search for a new, inclusive language of contemporary sensibility in all fields of art. In poetry, three of the important antecedents to Patchen's own discoveries were the works of Guillaume Apollinaire, the Italian futurists (especially F. T. Marinetti), and the dadaists.

Patchen knew the work of Apollinaire, one of the earliest major innovators of contemporary poetic forms. As early as 1912, the French poet referred to the mass media as a source of themes and techniques for poetry:

> I believe I have found a source of inspiration in prospectuses . . .
> catalogues, posters, advertisements of all sorts. Believe me, they
> contain the poetry of our epoch. I shall make it spring forth.
> >   (quoted in Roger Shattuck, *The Banquet Years*)

IL PLEUT

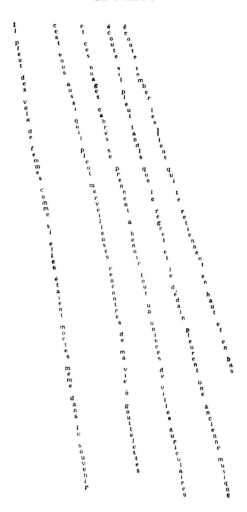

Apollinaire saw that the daily newspaper presents a format of simultaneity through the juxtaposition of totally incongruous events and images on a page, related to each other in a dual sense: temporally, by having occurred within the same twenty-four hours, and spatially, by existing on the same visual plane—the page.

Apollinaire was the first important modern poet to experiment with the size, shape, and placement of words in order to dissociate language from linear, discursive logic. In his *Calligrammes* he established the integration of the verbal and the visual in modern poetry. One is shown above.

19

Of the Italian futurists, the poet F. T. Marinetti was especially inventive in exploring the visual organization of the page through the use of varied typefaces mixed with handlettering.

Perhaps the most pervasive device of the dadaists, the one which most markedly set their activities apart from traditional "serious" art, was their deliberate cultivation of humor as a major vehicle of ideas. Dada accepted and exploited contradictions, giving form to the ambiguity of experience by using the compositional technique of chance manipulation of a mixture of disparate elements. Three Kurt Schwitters broadsides are shown above.

In one of his Dada manifestoes Tristan Tzara offered the following recipe:

To make a dadaist poem
Take a newspaper.
Take a pair of scissors.
Choose an article as long as you are planning to make your poem.
Cut out the article.
Then cut out each of the words that make up this article and put them in a bag.
Shake it gently.
Then take out the scraps one after the other in the order in which they left the bag.
Copy conscientiously.
The poem will be like you.
And here you are a writer, infinitely original and endowed with a sensibility that is charming though beyond the understanding of the vulgar.

Out of all of this avant-garde mixture, Patchen drew his own particularly humane blend of sense and non-sense and placed himself within that European tradition. But his relationship to this rich source of new language and ideas was an ambivalent one.

Central to the modernist philosophy, in all of the major movements, was the demand that art be *free*, just as the human spirit must be free. This was the legacy of the great Romantic rebellion against the materialistic bourgeois spirit of the nineteenth century. The romantics usually defined freedom in personal terms as the freedom to become fully oneself, unrestrained by the dogmas, customs, and institutions of society—a definition certainly close to Patchen's temperament.

For many American artists in the 1930s, however, the European aesthetic and intellectual inventions appeared to be frivolous indulgences. A number of European artists and writers were living as refugees in New York at the time and seemed to be carrying on some private game, dealing in cryptic symbols and forms, unrelated to the difficult American realities of the time.

In his second book, *First Will & Testament* (1939), Patchen's ambivalence toward the avant-garde is indicated in one of the three pieces written in theatrical form. In a book of new and maturing styles of writing, these pieces featuring the imperturbable Mr. Kek are a radical departure from the poems in *Before the Brave*, certainly in form if not in content. After some words in one of the pieces about the executions at the Salem witch trials of 1692, interspersed with dialogue about the Moscow purges of the 1930s, comes the following:

22

SHERNSH (*reading as one in a dream with a cold leg growing out of his neck*): The poem that I am about to read now has been hailed on both sides of the Atlantic (and in the middle) as a contribution to our culture. Axel Gaspard has said of it: "It causes blue monkeys to shine in my third eye."
Give me absolute quiet.
(*reads*)

POEM IN SIX DIMENSIONS OR TOMMY TOMMY'S MONOCHORD

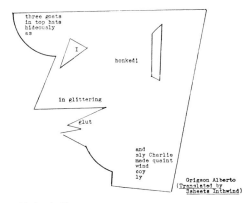

MIGA (*as crowd is hushed*):

A DAY IN THE LIFE OF A GREAT ARTIST, HURRIED

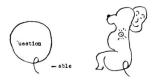

NOLLY (*with quite a lot of intensity*):
TWELVE FEATHERS filthy WITH BLOOD
OR
PUDDING

Is eated
By eve-
Ry one
But

I enjoy
Most!
Moose
On the
Half horn

JOHN LAW (*eagerly*): Is their work available?
MR. KEK: Tired of toilet walls?

23

This is the first time that Patchen presented in his writing a visual element beyond typeset words, and, as such, it may logically be considered a first step in the direction of the picture poems. It is the only pictorial element in the book, a form which Patchen will strongly expand in the future, yet it is curious that he both mocks his source ("Tired of toilet walls?") and builds his whole piece on its devices. Both the source and the technique are Dada, as is even the specific reference provided in one of the nonsensical footnotes which Patchen helpfully adds to "assist the reader to a better understanding of this work":

> 6. Annals of Kiki Mertz. Birthdate uncertain: Nason Prut (student of Egyptian Arseology) sets it at not later than 1347; Gonov, assistant to Poqybt (curator of Hennose Hyr) declares for 1437; Kiki says 1921. Her real name was Rossi Capellanus.

Kiki was a well-known model and a companion of avant-garde artists in Montparnasse; Mertz refers to Merz, a term used by Kurt Schwitters for his own version of Dada. The goofy humor, the pretense of significant meanings and erudition, mixed with scatological references, are part of the Dada arsenal of weapons aimed at bourgeois respectability. Patchen here mimics Dada even as he ridicules it.

24

The Journal of Albion Moonlight, Patchen's first full-length prose book and probably his best known work, was written in late 1939 and in 1940, while Europe, country by country, was falling to Hitler's armies. It is a book often described as surrealistic and is indeed a strange and haunted record of flight and search in a world of nightmares, though no more incredible and bizarre than the record of the Second World War. Patchen, writing down his vision of anguish as prophecy, was overtaken by events. Paris fell before the book was finished.

While this book shares the surrealist sense of dislocation (as in dreams) through convulsive imagery and violent contrast of tone and meaning, Patchen seems to dissociate himself from the surrealist movement. Two-thirds of the way through the book Albion Moonlight confronts the reader's potential accusation—that his testament may be merely an exercise in gratuitous aesthetic effects, without meaning or purpose:

> I exaggerate nothing. I am not a dealer in distortions. This is precisely the way I found the world. Imaginative people end by becoming tongue-tied. They talk above things. I operate from the inside. My feet never leave the ground. It is not my business that now and then the ground sinks away. I am heavy with the stars in my cap. I bring the sea in. I do no research whatever. Every problem to me is a problem of living. I make no attempt to translate. My speech is as much a part of my body as my arms and legs are. What have I to do with the cult of hallucination? Derangement is for the too-sane—everything under heaven cries to be *arranged;* I demand order and precision in what I do. The supreme cultivation of chaos has already been done. *That is what I am talking against.*

Patchen, speaking through Albion, again qualifies his involvement with the avant-garde, in this case with Surrealism. "Derangement" and "the cult of hallucination" must surely refer to the theories and practices of this dynamic and influential movement of the thirties, as well as to the war, "the supreme cultivation of chaos." By the late thirties Surrealism had become something of a fad, a veneer of styles and effects, practiced by a large group of lesser artists and writers, though its initial masters still continued their work. It is this cult that Patchen seems to reject, while his work shows his indebtedness to the spiritual concerns of Surrealism as well as to some of its artistic techniques.

We show selections from *The Journal of Albion Moonlight* on the following pages as Patchen had them set in type in the published book. But he wrote *Albion Moonlight,* as he wrote all his other works, by hand; he never composed on the typewriter. His manuscripts, thousands of individual sheets of paper covered by a handwriting reminiscent of a schoolchild's first mastery of script, before adult carelessness or perhe struck wildly about, his fists colliding with—nothing. He sank weakly into a chair.

TO SHAKE

"Open your eyes, Albion," a voice said. "What . . . ?" he murmured stupidly. For the first time he realized that his eyes were bandaged tightly shut. Desperately he tore at the thin strips of cloth, which came away

HANDS

in his fingers like frozen cobwebs. He looked about him now. Jenny was standing at the bar in deep talk with a man whose head was shrouded in a cheap, paper goat-mask such as children wear at Hallowe'en. Or so Albion assured himself: it was perhaps demanding too much to believe

NOW AND

that the creature was indeed half man and half goat. Across from him sat a group of little bearded men—more than twenty at the one table—they were spinning their white and red whiskers about like agitated skirts on their chins, and their thin voices scampered around in

WHEN

the tobacco smoke like baby mice in balls of wool. Every little while one of them would reach into his trousers and jerk wildly, the others simultaneously rocking and bounding with his movement. At such times the chief actor of

we can't look look look look look look look look look look
open up I freely confess, I am in agony I am afraid I have
enough lost my way LOOK AT ME look look look look at me
can't you look look look look look look look look look look
see? look look Here I am look look look look look look
I lift look look look look look look look! look! look!
my mask look! look! look! look! look! look! look! look!
ever look! look! look! look! do you see me! look! look!
so look! look! look! look! look! look! look! look!
little look! help me! help me! God help me! look! look!
do you look! look! look! look! look! look! look! look!
know me! look! look! look! look! look! look! look! look!

out of the womb . . . to stand crying
the ladies are all dead   A bloody cigar
the white ladies are sleeping under the hill   was found near
the ladies I say are all dead   the scene of the
what has happened to the white ladies?   crime. I don't
the poor ladies who dropped us out of   smoke cigars—
their bellies?   do you?
our mothers, eh lad? are sleeping under the dark hill
This is the sound of terror, this is the truth, this is the . . .
LOOK! LOOK! I am standing beside you
      a
      thin
I got up this morning   *wisp*   Please look at me, don't
with a headache and a   *of smoke*   slink away
feeling of bad fortune   curls from
just ahead. Several peo-   the black hole
ple dropped in during   in my temple
the day with news of one
thing and the other. It   What a damn nuisance: the laundry
appears that England   got my clothes confused with those of
will resist quite stub-   a small-time gangster (and I had to
bornly after all. I read   wear the stuff because I have only one

sonal idiosyncrasy slur or refine it, have very much the look of old, found writing. They possess a strong visual presence, the words as image apart from literal connotations. With the work clearly and completely in his mind, he wrote over sustained stretches of time, without outlines, corrections, or rewrites. This intensity of involvement was characteristic of Patchen's personality.

Patchen did not associate with organizations or movements, whether political or artistic. An open and generous man, he was nevertheless a loner by temperament,

I cannot remain silent. There is something I must tell you. I have a knife in my hand but I won't kill anyone. There is a road through the pale water and you and I can walk together for nobody will

care to kill
us because
we have done
nothing to
cause pain
or death or
despair to
any of our
fellows have
we please God
have we ever
wished harm
to any human
being I tell
you that there
will be an
accounting
and the streets
will flow blood
and the hills
will echo their
cries as we
torture them
for killing us

T
h
i
s

i
s

t
h
e

r
o
p
e

criticorum: genus irritabile vatum: to kalon: monumentum aere perennius (put me in the tomhouse). My melenemesis wound! The shrouded radiance . . . passive . . . humble . . . harnessed flesh

SYNCOPATED ecstasy
I DO NOT BELIEVE IN DEATH
horror— I pr $41X^2$ will

AUGUST 27 A savagely cold moon shines down on me as I move across the deep meadow which leads to the house of the Savior. I am no longer afraid. I shall not be lost ever again.

White slabs of living marble border my path. They gleam like teeth in the fat, sorrowful light. I think of the mocking head-stones which mark the graves of the mad and the hunted.

This is what I have reached . . .

I hurry; stumbling and sobbing that all the pain will soon be done. The thick watermoon tosses on the curved horns of cloud.

Splintered throats of angels drip their wounded blood on the highroad where the stars walk.

The shine of the moon is fish.

Small eyes looking out of me. The rustle of my mouth in the shadow cast by this time . . .

I can see the house now. As I watch, jabbering like an idiot, all the lights go on, and in every window—glory to God!—the face of Christ looks out.

a man fiercely pursuing his individuality both in life and in his work. The multiplicity and complexity of his style, the shifts of tone and mood, were achieved within a singularly stable and private life, dedicated unequivocally to one activity: his work. Not even Patchen's illness, which increasingly incapacitated him, could diffuse this focus. If anything, it increased and intensified it.

Working on his pages, Patchen made the *look* of his writing an aspect of its form, a visible record of the words in his mind, made concrete, living on paper, outside

footsteps of the beast seven wings!!
Breathe the wild air
O lovely earth! not DEATH
& the perfumed milk of my ladies
O flaming cave To be pure
Concealing tears   sleep
everything is like looking into a lepers mouth

Monday. Is this Monday? WHAT REALITY ARE YOU TALKING ABOUT
You won't leave me, will you? will you? will you? will you? will
you? will you? will you? will you?

One two three four five six seven sun blue tree door alive sticks
heaven eight hate nine thine ten amen and there wasn't a dry eye
in the house.

CHAPTER VI

The day sat on the window sill and combed sunbeams out of its
whiskers. It was as peaceful as an empty jug. Moonlight stretched
himself out flat before the altar. He prayed for a long time. When
he got back to his study the shadows were already playing hide-
and-seek on the foreheads of the numerous whores who paced
back and forth like grim cats in the streets below. He turned to his
journal and reread his entries of that summer. An eye looked over
his shoulder and made a cruel judgment.

the poet yet of the poet. The handwriting was a personal extension of the poet in
the way that a typed page with its mechanical and impersonally printed characters
would not have been. In *The Journal of Albion Moonlight*, where Patchen allowed his
handwriting to appear in the printed text for the first time, though only on one page
(shown above), its effect is startling, the handwritten script insisting on the personal,
the direct, the actual presence of the writer as a man, another rather obvious precur-
sor of the picture poems.

In *Cloth of the Tempest*, written in 1941, Patchen presented a wide range of visually oriented poems, no longer in mockery of Dada or surrealist works but as his own contribution in the tradition of Apollinaire.

These are poems which, by integrating visual and verbal elements into an organic whole, allowed Patchen to present conflicting elements in an immediate, compact format. As with the work of Apollinaire and the dadaists, linearity is broken, logical sequence is bypassed, and the reader/viewer is forced into the role of active participant in the experience of forming the poem.

30

HOW TO BE AN ARMY

 MANY SHOES   POTATOES   FLAGS & FLEAS

 RIFLES   TRENCHES   DETERMINATION

》》》》》》》》》》》》》》》》》》》》》》》
KNOWLEDGE OF MARCHING

$$\frac{58207}{27850} = \textbf{BLOOD}$$

\+ (GENERALS)

AND A FAITH IN THE RIGHT

† † † † † † † † † † † † † † † † † † †
† † † † † † † † † † † † † † † † † † †
† † † † † † † † † † † † † † † † † †
† † † † † † † † † † † † † † † † † †
† † † † † † † † † † † † † † † †

June 17, 1943

THE MURDER OF TWO MEN BY A YOUNG KID
WEARING LEMON-COLORED GLOVES

Wait.

    Wait.

                  Wait.

Wait.

  Wait.

                     Wait. Wait.

        Wait.

            Wait. Wait. Wait. Wait.

    Wait.

Wait.

    Now.

A comparison of two poems, written ten years apart, shows how Patchen's attention to visual composition and to the reader's involvement with the look of the page gave increased force and life to his later poetry.

The following is the first section from a short poem, "1935," published in *Before the Brave*, (1936):

> The guilt of man does not defer the sun.
> The sky sends out no S.O.S., the rivers
> Reconcile the valley-seed to villages
> Removed from priestly murders in our streets
> Flowers ask no mercy, needing none,
> Though stained by blood of pickets.
> The lynch-tree sends out its shoots
> Above the stripped slain body of the Negro.
> And the stars witness only the horror of space.

Here are Patchen's dual concerns, related in time and space, yet on separate planes— the counterpoint of life in nature and homicide. Here the form of the poem flows, though the contents may jolt.

men are getting scairt of their world. Charlie Hearse is hobbling your

way and the promised awa

THE NATURE OF REALITY

Bed.   Apple.

Sly bird.   Policeman.

Famine.   Rod of milk.

Dice.   Groan.

Stone.   Towel.

Divot.

"Put some on mine."   Six or Tad Prichard.

THE REALITY OF NATURE

Seeking

death   life

growth   decay

peace   madness

conflict   silence

birth   dissolution

"Put some in me."   Tad Prichard or none.

T   R R O R
  E

Ten years later, from *Panels for the Walls of Heaven* (1946), comes the page above.

The duality has been expanded into an emblematic general formula, inclusively multileveled yet conceptually clear and direct. The technique which makes this possible is obvious: the page is treated visually, the words interrelated in space rather than in grammatical context. The more one looks at the page, the more it yields in structural refinement and references. TERROR OR ERROR. "Put some on mine." "Put some in me." Capitals and periods in the top section—fragmenting, isolating elements; lowercase, unpunctuated, free words in the lower section. Two halves of a whole, symmetrical yet unequal. Patchen accepted the evidence of opposites, of contradictions, but his choice, his primary value, was always clear:

> I am a poet of life.
> What are we going to do?
> Where can we turn?
> There is so much hate in the world.
> I would crawl a thousand miles on my hands and
>   knees if that would stop the war.
>   (from *Albion Moonlight*)

Sleepers Awake, written in 1945, was an even further elaboration of Patchen's quest to make his writing comprehensive and alive. Probably his most complex and formally innovative work, it is a book of prose as poetry and poetry as prose, a book of driving contrasts of language and thought, a book in which sacred and profane, passionate and comic are contrapuntally intertwined to keep the reader constantly alert and actively engaged in the unfolding of Patchen's vision of life. The visual elements, typographical as well as pictorial, are integrated into the overall structure of the book rather than being restricted to single-page compositions. A six-page sequence is here shown.

34

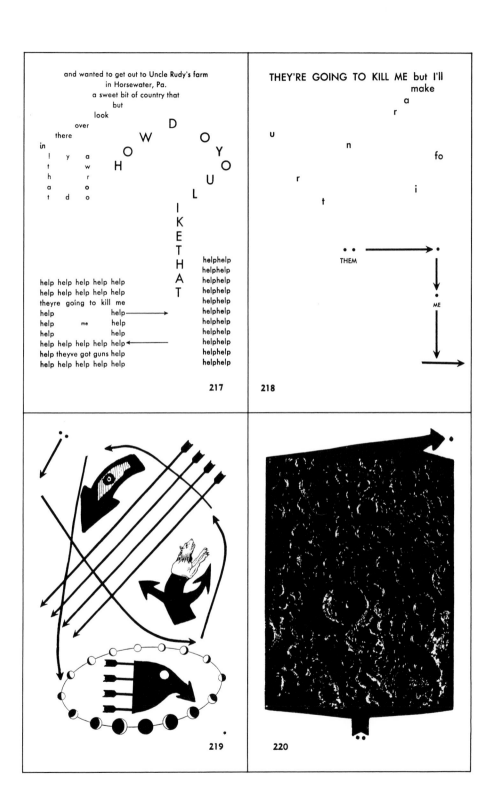

and wanted to get out to Uncle Rudy's farm
in Horsewater, Pa.
a sweet bit of country that
but
look
over
there
in
! y a H O W D O Y O U
t w r O O
h r U
a o L
t d o I
K
E
T
H
A
T

help help help help help   helphelp
help help help help   helphelp
theyre going to kill me   helphelp
help   help——→ helphelp
help   me   help   helphelp
help   help   helphelp
help help help help help←— helphelp
help theyve got guns help   helphelp
help help help help help   helphelp

217

THEY'RE GOING TO KILL ME but I'll
make
a
r
u
n
fo
r
i
t
THEM •• ——→ •
ME

218

219

220

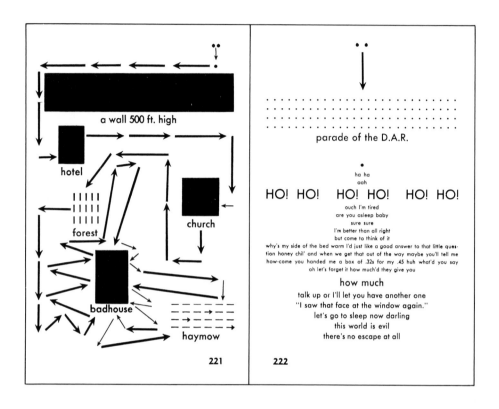

a wall 500 ft. high

hotel

forest

church

badhouse

haymow

221

parade of the D.A.R.

ha ha
aah

HO! HO!   HO! HO!   HO! HO!

ouch I'm tired
are you asleep baby
sure sure
I'm better than all right
but come to think of it
why's my side of the bed warm I'd just like a good answer to that little question honey chil' and when we get that out of the way maybe you'll tell me
how-come you handed me a box of .32s for my .45 huh what'd you say
oh let's forget it how much'd they give you

how much

talk up or I'll let you have another one
"I saw that face at the window again."
let's go to sleep now darling
this world is evil
there's no escape at all

222

After *Sleepers Awake,* Patchen concentrated on shorter forms. His increasing physical disability, caused by a spinal injury in 1937, prevented his undertaking long, sustained projects. In 1947 the Patchens left New York and for two and a half years lived in the small town of Old Lyme, Connecticut. There, in May 1950, confined to his bed and in constant pain, Patchen dictated *Fables and Other Little Tales* to Jonathan Williams, who was to publish them in 1953. The mood of these little pieces is openly funky and whimsical, witty rather than sardonic. It was a shift from the frantic nightmare worlds, the anguish and anger of many of his earlier works, and opened a new world of friendly, homey Patchen persons and critters who would eventually inhabit the picture poems.

Painted Books

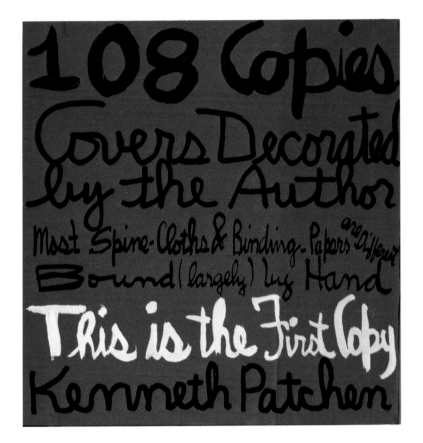

In THE WINTER of 1941 Patchen made the first in a continuing series of hand-painted covers for special limited editions of his published books. He individually designed, fabricated, signed, and numbered each cover and eventually made over one thousand volumes: nine separate titles, ranging from fifty to one hundred fifty unique covers for each. Within this vast range Patchen experimented with all kinds of paper and board supports, various glues and pigments (inks, watercolors, casein, cheap fabric dyes, and Japanese earth dyes), bits of applied paper and string and a non-repetitive, apparently inexhaustible host of designs and personages which paralleled his astonishing powers of discovery in the language of words.

From an interview between Miriam Patchen and Peter Veres in 1974:

Miriam Patchen: The painted books—limited painted editions—started as purely an economic thing. *The Dark Kingdom* was going to be a very beautiful book. Two young people who were going to publish it discovered they didn't have enough money to do a really beautiful book—that is, very fine type, very good paper, and the best of the printers, Peter Bielenson of Walpole Press.

So Kenneth suggested a limited edition—a subscriber edition. This is again one of those things that comes through necessity, let's say. It took a little think-

ing. He couldn't approve of just charging more for a book because he had
signed it, so he came up with the idea of a better-looking different form for the
book—a box book. And then, thinking about it, he decided that perhaps a
painting—some decoration on the cover—each one different, making it a very
personal thing to each person who got the copy . . . He'd have one of a kind;
no one else would have one just like it. That's how the painted covers came out.

   When that worked and succeeded very well, and the limited editions were
completely sold and subscribed to, Kenneth became completely enamored of

that method of raising money, which is a vulgar way of stating it—of bringing forth money from a book. And so, for most of his books of poetry, even as he did with *Sleepers Awake* for prose, eventually he had separate editions printed at the same time, sometimes on the same paper and the same press but always bound differently from the trade edition—a small, limited edition for every book he did so that he would have a painted edition for each one of his books. We would pay for a separate edition, generally even on the same paper, but with different bindings from the trade edition. And he would in

some cases paint directly on the cover, on the boards of the book; in some
cases he would paste Japanese papers on the covers, and in some cases he
mounted new boards on the books or had very special elegant bindings on
handmade papers done.

Each of these brought him closer to developing something with his painting,
something that was uniquely Kenneth Patchen, because he was not doing
things in oils, he was not doing art work; he was doing his own little figures,
melding them with the covers.

In the last two decades of his life, Patchen seems to have created another country
tangential to, though sometimes overlapping, that of his earlier works, where Albion
Moonlight had journeyed. The new land was somehow less oppressive than the old,
without the constant violence and turmoil of the years dominated by the Second
World War. It was as if, in leaving New York in 1947, Patchen unburdened himself of the urban pressures so evident in his earlier works. This is not to say that his
concern about war diminished after 1950, but that in his work of the fifties and
sixties (beginning with the *Fables* of 1950, and including the silkscreen folios of
1955-56 and the picture poems of 1966 and 1968) Patchen spoke increasingly of
joy and beauty, humor and fun. Anger and despair at human cruelty and stupidity
are still evident but are no longer the dominant mood. With increasing battles
against his own physical pain, with increasing immobility and isolation, Patchen's
art turned, amazingly enough, to laughter. There is never a hint of personal pain in
his work. His pain was that of a witness sensitive to the suffering inflicted by humans
upon each other.

Miriam Patchen: I think that the war was always, of course, a heavy—and became even in recent years—a very heavy burden for him to bear. But he did point out that man, unfortunately in our world, was at war even when there wasn't a war. His *Moonlight,* for instance, was an attempt to warn people about the war. It was written as the war was coming. He knew that people had to hear the warning and they didn't hear it.

But the creatures (and I think, even at that, the *Fables*) have a great deal of the horror, but not in a surrealistic way, but in a sort of real way in the sadness. The *Fables* make me very sad when I read them. There's lots of fun in them, but for me they're very sad things.

His poems, even in later years, were very conscious of the horrors of the world. But, curiously enough, Kenneth always, even in the very beginning, had a great warmth and sense of humor and loved all living things, to the point where he'd do anything to keep, well, a mouse alive.

So it comes through. But then his creatures became more real. Possibly it was the Connecticut thing. We were surrounded by all kinds of immense dogs and little dogs and we had our cat, and we were very much living with creatures, which you can't do very much in New York City. So, in a curious way, we probably had more of a natural living starting in Connecticut with

the immense dogs and the little dogs and our little, little cat that was about two inches when we first got it; it went to sleep in the dog's mouth. So that could be...

And the dogs brought us rabbits, and that incident might have been one of the real things portrayed in a funny way with his creatures—when the large dog next door brought a rabbit to me one day. The rabbit was in the dog's mouth, and it was a very small rabbit. Not a hair on the rabbit was wet, and the dog brought this whole little live rabbit to me and just gave it to me. And then the cat sleeping in the dog's mouth on a hot day—that is in a sense, perhaps, a reality of some of Kenneth's creatures. I don't know...

Peter Veres: It's the kind of respect for and love for life untouched by greed, maybe, that allows for a representation of what might be. And the creatures are really creatures that might be.

M.P.: Yes. They *are.*

P.V.: And they are not the creatures on the landscape of *Albion Moonlight.* They really are from a different, possible world rather than an actual one.

M.P.: True, true.

P.V.: It just seems to me an amazing fact that Kenneth Patchen, who was increasingly suffering personal pain, started working in ways that gave more and more joy and pleasure, probably to himself in a way.

M.P.: Yes, he enjoyed it. Even though it was painful, he enjoyed it. There were many times we laughed when his creatures would look at us, oh yes.

P.V.: The humor which he always, I think, used as a tool of his art—not for comic relief, certainly, but as a deeper tool—also has a range. On a certain level, it can be very sardonic and ironic; certainly in *Memoirs of a Shy Pornographer* it's very ironic and cutting. I think that the humor in the picture poems—again with these critters—is much more mellow somehow; it doesn't have that edge to it; it's more a mellow kind of laughter.

M.P.: Yes. Was Kenneth trying to bind up his world's wounds a bit? I don't know. But he always had that warmth and love. Perhaps he felt that some of us needed this relief from pain—no, it wasn't that either. He just wanted to give something warm and loving.

46

Silkscreens

IN 1955 AND 1956, living in San Francisco, Patchen produced two portfolio editions of silkscreened poems with drawings. *Glory Never Guesses* and *A Surprise for the Bagpipe Player* is each composed of eighteen loose sheets printed on handsome Japanese paper. There are two hundred copies of each edition, totaling seventy-two hundred pages, printed by Patchen's old friend Frank Bacher, painter and silkscreen expert. Patchen not only made the original masters for each page but also hand-tinted with Japanese earth colors about five thousand of the prints to make up for the lack of color in the paper itself. This combination of screened and handpainted processes individualized most of the pages in a way similar to that of the painted books, and later the picture poems. The uniqueness of the gift-object was always significant for Patchen.

Miriam Patchen: Frank and Kenneth, being good old friends and admiring each other's work very much, came up with the idea that Frank would run off some silkscreens. "Now, you do them," said Frank. "You do whatever you want and I'll run them off." Kenneth was at the time pretty much bed confined, and yet this interested him very much. So he began to experiment with that peculiar film on which the thing is run. And he began to do the work directly onto the film, which would then be used as a pattern for the silkscreen. He was writing the words separately but doing drawings and patterns and designs onto the films, cutting them—not so much cutting them with a knife (that Frank eventually did)—but doing the black, heavy black, and then Frank would follow and cut it out for the silkscreen.

48

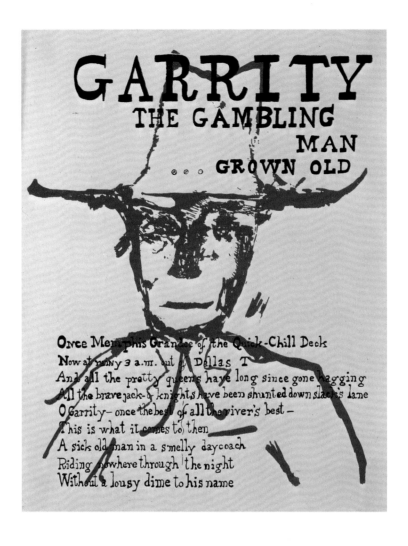

GARRITY
THE GAMBLING
MAN
... GROWN OLD

Once Memphis Grandee of the Quick-Chill Deck
Now at many 3 a.m. out of Dallas T
And all the pretty queens have long since gone bagging
All the brave jack-& knights have been shunted down slack's lane
O Garrity- once the best of all the river's best —
This is what it comes to, then
A sick old man in a smelly daycoach
Riding nowhere through the night
Without a lousy dime to his name

Kenneth got fine papers, but at that point the colored papers from Japan weren't so available. They got some very fine rice papers and ran two editions, two folios—*A Surprise for the Bagpipe Player* and *Glory Never Guesses;* they ran eighteen silkscreens separately for each of the two folios, some of them done in elaborate color and some in very little color but with the colored paper.

This, in a way, was illustration more than blending of words and designs or drawings. It's true that they loaned their qualities one to the other, but still it was more illustration than his later picture poems were.

With one tiny stick

To arrange the air over the eating-shed

And the evil part of the earth around it

So that at last

Not even the stick is left

Peter Veres: But it seems to be the midway point between the earlier work and the picture poems.

M.P.: Oh yes, that got him moving, got him interested and excited—seeing how it looked.

P.V.: The silkscreens themselves are relatively large, eleven by fourteen inches, and so in a way they get beyond the book size and have a real presence as a single image.

O honor the bird
That opened the word
That found the world
That love might live
O choose the wonder
That knelt on the water
That sun & wind made move
And Love O it shall flame
Though darkness quell every name

P.V.: Were they designed initially as a folio of single pages, or was there any other purpose in mind?

M.P.: Designed initially as a folio of single pages. We had a few run off on pure white very transparent paper—and double fold, French fold, so that we could do a volume so that they wouldn't disappear forever. And the silkscreens were run with just the colored type and on those pages, so we have a few volumes of those. But the single pages were the original idea.

IN BACK OF

EVERY REALLY THOUGHTFUL CHICKEN

Is some motherly egg or other
Smiling chalkily (although bald)
~Until it gets popped into a pan

Or mauled by a train or marauding elk
But from the leg of that hickory tree
A dappled little pelican beams down on me

P.V.: Then that really gets to his notion of the page outside the book because a purchaser would be able to do whatever with those single pages.

M.P.: Correct. And some people have put them on glass on their windows or covered an entire wall—a friend has covered an entire wall with separate silkscreen prints.

P.V.: And here in your living room you have them on a folding screen . . . .

The Picture Poems

Although patchen's drawings of beasties and critters dated back to the 1950s, appearing on the handwritten pages of poetry in his silkscreen folios, it was only in the picture poems of the sixties (published by New Directions in black and white in *Hallelujah Anyway,* 1966, and *But Even So,* 1968) that the images and words achieved a truly integrated union, a symbiosis.

Patchen's picture poems are magical, or, perhaps more properly, "fantastic." They are messages from another land, spoken in our vernacular by vaguely familiar creatures. Figures and words share a continuum of visual presence and form a counterpoint of meaning, an interchange of energies. Words as images, images as concepts, co-existing without subservience to each other, are combined to create a richer whole.

Patchen made nearly two hundred of these picture poems, all on very old off-white handmade paper, with uneven, uncut edges, all about eleven and a half by seventeen inches, which gives the impression of found, ancient manuscripts. Present in each of them is the spirit of the intensely personal and the intensely direct gift.

Miriam Patchen: It's like so many things—inventors work all their lives on trying to do something. The thing they're doing doesn't happen and yet accidentally something else happens, and they discover or create something they hadn't planned on.

In a way, this is almost what happened with Kenneth's picture poems and painting poems. When he was very uncomfortable in Palo Alto, bedfast and trying to do things, John Thomas, who is now and was then in the Department of Botany at Stanford, brought us, almost accidentally, some very strange old papers.

Kenneth always loved beautiful paper, lovely types, good books. But these very strange old papers were handmade, of great, great age. They were at Stanford and were used to press, or had been holding, botanical specimens that had come from France many, many years ago. Some of the papers literally went back to the days of Napoleon's army, and John Thomas was rather shocked when he discovered that the paper was being thrown away and burned when they were reclassifying their botanical specimens. So he, too, was interested in paper and had a little press, and he and Kenneth decided that they might do a couple of Christmas cards on the paper or something like that. But he brought the paper to Kenneth, and Kenneth was just really so fascinated by the paper he would pore over it and pet it and look at it night after night when he couldn't do anything else. Gradually he began to think that it would be a terrible waste not to do something desirable with the paper. Fine to do the Christmas cards and some printing, yes, but this paper should exist, and continue to exist, because it could; since it was pure rag paper, it could continue to exist for some purpose other than just being around.

54

55

Caring is the only daring oh you know it

Patchen

56

IN PERKKOS GROTTO

Everybody
Gets along
Just fine
Why
Even
The best
Champagne
Tastes like elderberry wine!

Patchen

58

He experimented a little with this and a little with that and gradually tested it with color, and that began to intrigue him more and more. And began to make him think of painting on the paper and doing color. Then color began to open up his mind to putting color in a sense visually into his poetry. That led to painting on the papers.

He did some black drawing pages on some of the paper, but still that wasn't satisfactory enough for the paper's honor. So gradually the painting forms evolved because of these papers.

Peter Veres: I was always intrigued by the fact that you found some buttons or something in a paper at—

M.P.: What we call common pins—the ones with the little head, the straight pin with the head? He found original handmade ones that don't have a head, but have a funny little hook on the end, that go way, way back before we had common pins. And he found some pieces of the herbs and leaves that had been pressed and the markings, and he found on a couple of the sheets some shopping lists that were obviously written down by someone who took care of the military supplies of those days.

P.V.: In Napoleon's time.

M.P.: Yes. Kenneth had nights of fascinated pleasure with those papers. But then every single sheet was exactly the same size as the other. There were some darker ones and some lighter ones, and Kenneth separated the lighter ones for the painting poems and so on. Some were really beautiful, had marvelous watermarks on them and were magnificent papers. But then he would find a batch, every one apparently identical. And yet, if you used some material on number one sheet, the second sheet would absolutely reject everything he tried to put on it.

60

62

Come now, my child

if we were
to harm you, planning
we'd be lurking here
beside the path
in the very dark-
est part of
the forest?

Patchen

The Hands of the Air

applaud the Wonders of God O Light & Life unending

Patchen

64

THE BEST HOPE

Is that one of these days the ground will get disgusted enough just to walk away — leaving people with nothing more to stand on than what they have so bloody well stood for up to now

Patchen

65

P.V.: He painted on them and he wrote on them and he sometimes pasted objects—pieces of paper or candy wrappers or whatever to make a kind of collage of personages.

M.P.: Correct.

P.V.: This was a habit he had already established when he was doing the book covers—the painted books . . .

M.P.: It's true, he had done a little of the pasting on of the painted books, not too often, but he had experimented a couple of times. He'd use string and things like that.

P.V.: Yes. I remember some were heavily pasted up with objects. Since this was really the first time he approached the page as a painting with poetry (whereas the book jackets were really just pictures to decorate the book as a cover), it might be interesting to ask, "Did he do the writing on another page before he approached that picture poem page, or did he actually write and compose it for that page and then put the pictures on, or were they all different approaches?"

M.P.: I like your use of the word "compose" at that point because people often ask, or probably very often have asked someone who was connected with a song, whether the words or the music came first. In this case I'm not very helpful—I would say it was one or the other. It's true that when he was doing the figures of the paintings he had immediately an idea in his head of what they were going to be involved with. He did write the words on another piece of paper separately, generally not before, but they probably were in his head all the time, as all his poems were. But then he often wrote them onto another paper just to see about the placement of the words in connection with a figure. I think generally they were in almost identical development in the head—the figure and the words.

66

67

an interview with THE FLOATING MAN

But if you see no hope at all, isn't it sort of.. well, a lie — all your talk about how human beings must love one another?

Yes, my friend, it is a lie. Already on the calendar blazes the moment of all-freeing Truth.. of Peace & Brotherhood of Equality & Integration – an end to misery and fear and hatred

Why, in that wonderful moment even their skins (had they skins) will be a quite acceptable color of cinder-black

Patchen

68

AND TO THINK ·· IT ALL Start-ed Out LIKE ANY Other

Peace or we all perish World

for miriam · on our twenty-eighth wedding Anniversary 28 June 92

Kenneth Patchen

Intended, one might almost have been led to believe, to last for a good long time

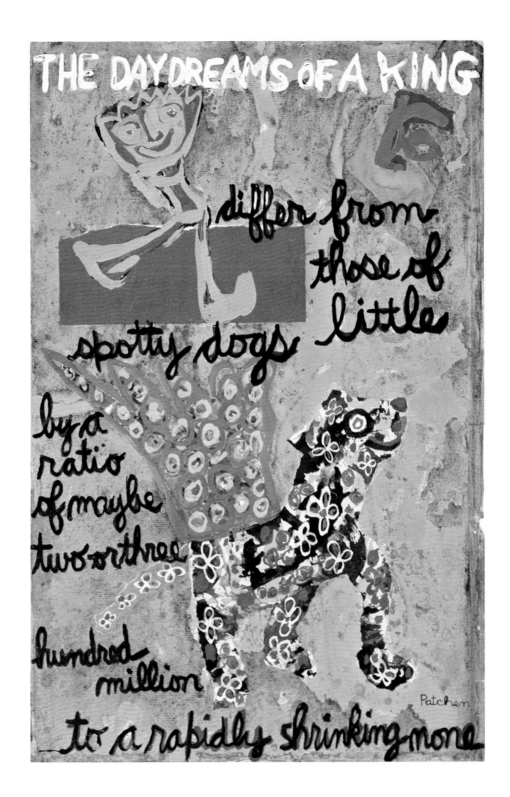

THE DAYDREAMS OF A KING

differ from those of little spotty dogs by a ratio of maybe two or three hundred million to a rapidly shrinking none

Patchen

P.V.: And this was, of course, a period of time when he was really in pain and was hard put to do this work.

M.P.: Yes.

P.V.: And he did them mostly on the bed.

M.P.: He did them all on the bed, and it did cause physical trouble for him to do it because he couldn't sit and he couldn't stand, and lying on his left side was very painful. But since he was right-handed, he had to pretty well lie on his left side when he was writing. Sometimes it was sort of an odd position. But even at that—painful as it was—it gave him a change from thinking about and writing straight writing, and it was a change of air for him. He would like to have been able to stand up to work at a table or workbench. There's no question that his condition determined the direction of some of his art.

P.V.: Having such limited strength also might have made it possible to work on one page at a time where it wasn't possible to work on a long, extended project. We know from the picture poems that they are in fact designed as individual pages rather than as a run or a sequence . . .

M.P.: True, true. These were a relief because he knew he could do in a fairly short time—as a matter of fact, a very short time—each one, whereas an extended book he couldn't take on. That's why those books don't exist that had been announced, because he just didn't dare go into something that would take longer.

P.V.: Once you spoke about Kenneth's interest in having a page have a presence in the way that an object, a page of poetry, something that comes out of the book, is part of your household, sits on a table and is itself. This notion, I think you said, came also with that sense of having Christmas cards or some kind of gift of this sort—have it stand out and be. Would you think the picture poems were close to that in his mind?

M.P.: Yes, I think they're very close to that, and they undoubtedly developed from that because he had hoped to do poems for the table. As you know, we did some postcards—had some postcards done for us with drawings and so on. Kenneth always planned on something that stood, similar to some of the calendars that people have.

72

I AM THE GHOST OF

Chief Mountain-Lyin'
(Since-Everyone-Else-Is)

I wedded
Pretty
Red Wing
and if you don't
believe it,
right
down there's
our daughter,
Bob

Lucky
you made
no deposit
on the country
—just throw
it
away
when you're
finished
with
it

Patchen

74

Patchen constructed his picture poems in two basic ways. In one, the figures are framed in small rectangles on the page and are thus separated from the painted words which flow outside the compartments. The rectangles, usually only one or two to a page, may be painted around the figures, or they may be made up from pieces of painted-on paper to be pasted on the page. The latter method suggests a found fragment—preserved, presented, and commented on by the text.

In Patchen's other method of arrangement, the figures have full freedom on the page—unframed, floating among, through (and sometimes under), the script. These tend to be the most fluid compositions, the script allowed the greatest freedom to change direction, size and form. The compartmentalized pages are more stable, more reserved and Patchen mixed the two methods on some of his painted pages. Each picture poem is a distinctive entity, a world sufficient to itself, somehow related to all the others but not in a sequential or a narrative way.

The creatures themselves are formed of bits of torn and painted papers, of blots and scribbles, casual silhouettes nudged into life by the addition of an eye or two in the appropriate places, some feet, perhaps feathers, ears, horns, or beaks. They are a gentle folk, sometimes smiling but mostly just standing around, *being*. They are not active. Many of them have no arms or hands. They are simply *there*, in their world of the page, as presences. In most of the picture poems Patchen shows only two or three beings, rarely more. Their often prominent heads and attitudes of apparent conversation are reminiscent of puppets—ancient and magical beings speaking from small closed stages to an intimate audience willing to suspend disbelief. Puppets, unlike actors in the naturalistic theater, have merely to present themselves to be believed. They need no settings, no personal histories, no psychological explanations. Patchen presents his little beasties in a stage of words.

All Are Animals
You know that trees are animals like any others; just as flowers and lakes—and even what we think and what we say, what we dream, what we imagine—these too are animals, animals like any others. And stars, and sky, the moon, the sun, the earth—oh, yes, these too! all are animals!

Poemscape (146)

78

THE WALKER STANDING

If your return Before you go

Most fist-shuffles Will seem pretty slow

Patchen

81

Patchen's figures exist in wordscapes. The words, which are the poems, animate the spaces around and about the creatures, setting visual counterpoints with them. The lettering is as varied and direct as the figures—the directness that of a child totally engaged in making a picture with a story intertwined in the open spaces. An analogy to children's art is as inescapable with Patchen as it is with Klee and Miró. Young children build their world of forms out of limited but variable and highly suggestive visual elements, where small modifications and accents beget person or beast, tree or sun. Patchen's figures resemble the style of a six- or seven-year-old, consciously experimenting, evoking beings with control and invention, not yet inhibited by adult conventions. At about this age the child learns to write, and Patchen's writing, especially his script, does resemble that of a schoolchild. Carefully ruling his lines in pencil, he forms his letters as he has been taught, making every loop, keeping them as clear as he can. No adult scribbling, no accomplished flair, nothing slick, though at times the script breaks out of line and moves in various directions, changing size and color, as might graffiti on a wall.

Some of the picture poems are nearly monochromatic; others have a wide range of intense color. Those that appeared in black and white in *Hallelujah Anyway* are works of very diverse color moods, while the later *But Even So* pieces all share a pervasive soft ochre luminosity. As it was for Blake, "energy is eternal delight" for Patchen. These works project a crude vitality rather than a measured beauty. Not pretty or sentimental, cool or elegant, they are direct and personal, involved in the process of making, and they show as evidence the marks of the tools, effacing nothing, building the page into a whole image of contained energy.

In his last years, from which the picture poems date, Patchen was in great pain and bedridden. These works, large enough to project a robust presence but easily encompassed by a gesture of the hand, are intimate and direct worlds to be approached within arm's length.

In his last years, from which the picture poems date, Patchen was in great pain and bedridden. These works, large enough to project a robust presence but easily encompassed by a gesture of the hand, are intimate and direct worlds to be approached within arm's length. In *But Even So* he wrote:

> Alas I remember most what never happened —
> I am not a silver-bearded king nor yet am I any man's slave.
> My fist against all enemies of life.
> The light fills this room on the table a tiny bell,
> water glass, papers covered with writing
> The Human Winter—I Wonder What Ever Became of
>   Human Beings.
> a tiny bell   a waterglass   pens ink paints
>
> This room, this battlefield.

A
feeling
of
passionate
mercy

the rest
doesn't
matter
a damn!

Patchen

Sculptures

W HILE THE CREATURES of the picture poems were being born on the pages of Napoleonic rag papers, certain small sculpted critters joined Patchen's Palo Alto household.

Peter Veres: They're all about hand-holding size, would you say?

Miriam Patchen: That's a perfect description, unless you have a very small hand for that little bird.

P.V.: Right. And there's that lovely yellow bear. Would you like to speak a little bit about how these became?

M.P.: As I said, Kenneth was always very, very careful about everything, and some of the Napoleonic papers he trimmed for one reason or another, and sometimes he cut them up to get pieces for collage. But he couldn't bear to throw away any bit of it. In the beginning he had a little box filled with little scraps of the paper and it just bore down on him, this wonderful paper. So he decided that he would make some use of that marvelous paper. He began to

save it, and he created them; we created papier-mâché from Napoleonic paper putting a little bit of everything into it—yes, glue and paste and rice paste and carpenter's glue and a little bit of everything. But these are all papier-mâché, some of them *extremely* heavy; I can't imagine why, except because of the materials we used. He had planned to make quite a few sculptures . . .

There again, this was in a funny way a release from tensions, as his painting poems were—breaking it up into a change of pace. And he began to create his animals, his an-imals, and his little—his wonderful golden bear and his blue bear and ones you really can't describe. There's one that's extremely light; now why it has no weight at all . . . although it's small, it's very light. It's a little bird with a long red beak. Then there's one that is not much

86

larger, extremely heavy for its size. That one has something on it—who knows what it is? I sent for a tube of something that's supposed to make things look like pewter or silver, depending on how you use it, and this looks like pewter. But it became heavy. Then there is the golden bear which Peter Veres likes so much. That's one of Kenneth's golden bears.

P.V.: Of course, these are obviously so much first cousins or brothers to the critters in the picture poems that they seemingly have come to life on their own space and time. It's just, again, a wonderful personal presence of Kenneth Patchen's love of animals.

M.P.: Yes. The blue bear is laughing in a very friendly way; he's really laughing with great pleasure.

P.V.: There's very much of a folk quality—that is, unpretentious folk craft in these as well as in the picture poem paintings—not in the folk-craft tradition of obviously followed patterns and rules but in the almost amateur way of doing things for your own love instead of for sale or some commercial museum show.

M.P.: That is probably where Kenneth's thing comes from because Kenneth was very folk in a funny way. He was not cultured or academic or that way; he was folk. His grandparents had been in the Pennsylvania Dutch area, and the tales from his Scotch grandfather's songs and so on—this is probably where it comes from more really and more correctly than something else. Kenneth is folk rather than conventional educational systems.

P.V.: Folk has this sort of familiarity with concrete substances, the materials, which these little guys have, these little animules.

M.P.: An-imal. This one's name is An Imal.

P.V.: They're wonderful little creatures. They also, in a way, suggest again child images or child papier-mâchés; some that my kids have done seem to have the same quality—very direct and very simple. And simplicity and directness are, for me, the essence of many of the late picture poems. That doesn't mean that there is no sophistication and poetic insight, of course. But it's a directness, a very upfront folk presence and quality.

M.P.: Yes, that is the difference, the absolute directness, because Kenneth was always direct—in everything, in words and everything else. The only time he ever got angry at me was very brief. I'd said something to him about, "Well, you just say it in your writing, but I don't know if you believe this or this that much." And that was the only time he got angry. He said, "I've never told a lie. The one thing I despise is a lie." And that same directness in his work and in his little animals—that's the character of the man.

Kenneth Patchen: His Life

(a brief biography and selective bibliography prepared by Peter Veres and
Miriam Patchen)

1911   December 13, born in Niles, Ohio. His father was a steelworker;
        his grandfather had been a miner in Pennsylvania. His father was a
        Protestant, his mother a Catholic. One older brother, four younger
        sisters, two of whom died young.

1915   His family moved to Warren, Ohio, five miles from Niles, where he
        attended public schools. He was a member of the football, track, and
        debating teams and the school orchestra and newspaper.

1923   He started a diary and wrote daily from then on.

1928   Patchen first published poems in school magazines and in the New
        York *Times*. He worked in a steelmill on his father's crew in the
        summer after graduation from high school.

1929   Summer work in the steelmill. In the fall, entered Alexander
        Meiklejohn's Experimental College at the U. of Wisconsin on a
        scholarship. Studied there for one year.

1930   Attended Commonwealth College in Mena, Arkansas, for part of the
        year. He was on the road before and after, in assorted jobs—as
        gardener, janitor, rubber-factory worker—always writing.

1931-32 In New York City, writing and working. Attended writing classes
        briefly at Columbia. Worked near Amenia, N.Y. and at Killington
        Peak and the Green Mountain Trail, Vermont.

1933   In Boston, befriended by poets Conrad Aiken, John Wheelwright
        and others. Met Miriam Oikemus on Christmas Eve in Boston.
        She was 17, a freshman at Massachusetts State College, active in
        antiwar work, from a Finnish pacifist family.

1934   On June 28, he and Miriam were married in Sharon, Pa. Moved to
        New York, where he worked on the American Guide Series, a WPA
        writers' project.

1935   Summer in Rhinebeck, N.Y., writing most of *Before the Brave* for
        publication by Random House.

1936   *Before the Brave* (New York: Random House), poetry.

        Received a Guggenheim Fellowship in March. In April went to
        Santa Fe, New Mexico, to write. Stayed until November.

1937	In Hollywood, working as a "script doctor," also writing original film scripts. In the fall Patchen's back trouble began as a result of his trying to separate the locked bumpers of two cars which had collided. A doctor diagnosed his pain as arthritis. Writing *First Will & Testament.*
1938	Remained in Hollywood for part of the year, then to Los Angeles to work on the WPA guides. In bed for six weeks with back pain. Working on *First Will & Testament.* Sent by the state of California back to Miriam's family in Concord, Massachusetts. Met James Laughlin, founder of New Directions, who was interested in *First Will & Testament.* He invited the Patchens to work for the publishing company in Norfolk, Connecticut.
1939	*First Will & Testament* (Norfolk: New Directions), poetry.

Worked for New Directions. In the fall, moved to 81 Bleeker St., New York, to the loft where Herman Melville had lived. Began *The Journal of Albion Moonlight.* (The Patchens were to live in New York, with brief absences, for eight years, until 1947.) |
| 1941 | *The Journal of Albion Moonlight* (Mt. Vernon, N.Y.: Kenneth Patchen), prose.

Writing *Cloth of the Tempest* in New York and in Mt. Pleasant, N.Y. in the summer. Increasing physical discomfort. |
| 1942 | *The Dark Kingdom* (New York: Harriss and Givens), poetry. Included an edition of 75 copies with covers painted by K.P. (This was written while Patchen was living on Avenue A in New York, bedfast.)

The Teeth of the Lion (Norfolk: New Directions), a selection of poetry. |
| 1943 | *Cloth of the Tempest* (New York: Harper & Bros.), poetry. |
| 1944 | Writing *The Memoirs of a Shy Pornographer* and *They Keep Riding Down All the Time* in New York and *Pictures of Life and of Death* in Mt. Pleasant. |
| 1945 | *The Memoirs of a Shy Pornographer* (New York: New Directions), prose.

Living on West 12th St., New York, writing *Sleepers Awake.* Incapacitated in bed much of the time. When well enough, selecting type with the printer for *Sleepers Awake.* Working on *An Astonished Eye . . . .* |
| 1946 | *Sleepers Awake* (New York: Padell Book Co.), prose, with a limited edition of 75 painted books.

They Keep Riding Down All the Time (New York: Padell), poetry. |

Panels for the Walls of Heaven (Berkeley: Bern Porter), poems-in-prose with a limited edition of 150 painted books.

An Astonished Eye Looks Out at the Air (Walport, Oregon: The Untide Press), poetry.

Pictures of Life and of Death (New York: Padell), poetry.

The Selected Poems of Kenneth Patchen (Norfolk: New Directions).

Sporadic acute back pain. Some poetry readings at the New York Public Library and the Y.M.H.A. Miriam Patchen did filing work at New Directions' New York office and sales work at Macy's.

1947   Introduction to *Illustrations of the Book of Job by William Blake* (New York: United Book Guild).

The Patchens moved to Old Lyme, Connecticut, and lived there until 1950.

1948   *See You in the Morning* (New York: Padell), novel.

(Written in Old Lyme, *See You* was to be a popular novel for mass appeal, sold through Sears Roebuck, but Padell refused to participate in that marketing plan.) In 1948 and 1949, Patchen's first experiments in reading poetry to jazz recordings.

To Say If You Love Someone (Prairie City, Ill.: The Decker Press), selection of love poems with a subsequent unnumbered edition of painted covers (created from 1960 to 1970).

Red Wine & Yellow Hair (New York: New Directions), poetry, with a limited edition of 180 painted books.

1950   More severe problems with Patchen's back. In the summer he dictated *Fables* to Jonathan Williams in the Old Lyme cottage while bedridden in great pain. To raise money for medical care, a fundraising drive was begun, headed by T. S. Eliot, W. H. Auden, Archibald MacLeish, and Thornton Wilder and supported by poetry readings by Auden, MacLeish, Wilder, and Marianne Moore, William Carlos Williams, e.e. cummings, and Edith Sitwell. The surgery in the fall was a success and he was well for about two years. In the winter the Patchens moved to San Francisco where they lived on Green Street until 1955. During this time, Miriam worked as a salesclerk in San Francisco.

1952   *Orchards, Thrones and Caravans* (San Francisco: The Print Workshop), poetry.

Back problems returned, with increasing pain and disability, until an operation in 1956.

1953   *Fables and Other Little Tales* (Karlsruhe, Germany: Jonathan Williams), prose.

Worked with Frank Bacher's help on silkscreen portfolios.

1954   *The Famous Boating Party* (New York: New Directions), prose-poems with a limited edition of 50 painted books.

        Poems of Humor & Protest (San Francisco: City Lights), a selection of poetry.

        Received Shelley Memorial Award. Worked on the silkscreen portfolios. Miriam became ill.

1955   *Glory Never Guesses* (San Francisco: Kenneth Patchen), silkscreen portfolio—a collection of 18 poems with drawings on handmade Japanese papers, silkscreened by Frank Bacher. Two hundred copies.

        Miriam's illness diagnosed as multiple sclerosis. They moved to Palo Alto, California.

1956   *A Surprise for the Bagpipe Player* (San Francisco: Kenneth Patchen), silkscreen portfolio—18 more poems with drawings on handmade Japanese papers, silkscreened by Frank Bacher. Two hundred copies.

        A spinal fusion operation in Palo Alto during the summer was a total success. Absolute good health for the first time since 1937.

1957   *Hurrah for Anything* (Highlands, N.C.: Jonathan Williams), poems and drawings, with a limited edition of 100 painted books.

        When We Were Here Together (New York: New Directions), poetry with a limited edition of 75 painted books.

        In the fall, began readings of poetry with jazz ensembles in clubs in San Francisco and Los Angeles. Continued "poetry-jazz" until 1959.

1958   *Poem-scapes* (Highlands, N.C.: Jonathan Williams), prose-poems, with a limited edition of 75 painted books.

        The poetry and jazz readings continued in Los Angeles, Seattle and Vancouver. Miriam worked as a clerk until 1960, her illness now in remission.

1959   Patchen continued poetry readings with jazz groups. After two weeks in New York with Charlie Mingus in the fall, he came back to San Francisco for exploratory lung surgery at a doctor's insistence. During the operation an accident destroyed the successful results of the 1956 spinal fusion. He never recovered his health and remained bedridden in Palo Alto for the rest of his life. His only play, *Don't Look Now*, produced at Outside at the Inside in Palo Alto, opening on October 31 for a six-week run.

1960   *Because It Is* (Norfolk: New Directions), poems and drawings.

        The Moment (Palo Alto: Kenneth Patchen), a bound edition of the two silkscreen portfolios, *Glory Never Guesses* and *A Surprise for the Bagpipe Player*, limited to 42 copies, silkscreened by Frank Bacher and signed by Patchen.

For the next years, slow work on the picture poems at home in
Palo Alto.

1965   *Doubleheader* including *Hurrah for Anything, Poem-scapes* and
        A Letter to God (New York: New Directions), poems, prose-poems
        and drawings, widely available for the first time.

1966   *Hallelujah Anyway* (New York: New Directions), 88 pictures
        poems.

1967   Received a $10,000 award from the National Foundation of Arts and
        Humanities for his life-long contribution to American letters.

        The Collected Poems of Kenneth Patchen (New York: New
        Directions).

1968   *But Even So* (New York: New Directions), picture poems.

1970   *Aflame and Afun of Walking Faces* (New York: New Directions),
        fables and drawings. This was made up mainly of material from
        the 1953 *Fables* with drawings especially made in 1969 for this
        edition.

        In Quest of Candlelighters (New York: New Directions), a selection
        of prose-poems, drawings and a short story.

1971   *Wonderings* (New York: New Directions), basically a selection from
        earlier drawings, picture poems, and silkscreens. It was his last
        published book; he did not live to see it published.

1972   Kenneth Patchen died at home on January 2.

The Argument of Innocence was typeset by
Spartan Typographers in Plantin
Separations: American Color Corporation
Printing: Carey Colorgraphic Corporation
Binding: Roswell Bookbinding
Design: Daniel Gridley and Frederick Mitchell

The Press is grateful for the help of
Richard Schuettge, Ellen Bry, Janet Wilson,
Steve Clark, Jonathan Clark, and Jerry
Bragstad in making this book.

THE
WALKER
STANDING

If you return
Before you go

Most fast-shuffles
Will seem pretty slow

Patchen